GLASGOW URBAN MYTHS

GLASGOW URBAN MYTHS

IAN BLACK

BLACK & WHITE PUBLISHING

First published 2006
by Black & White Publishing Ltd
99 Giles Street, Edinburgh EH6 6BZ

ISBN 10:   1 84502 127 4
ISBN 13:   987 1 84502 127 6

British Library Cataloguing in Publication Data:
A catalogue record for this book is available
from the British Library.

Printed and bound by Nørhaven Paperback A/S

DEDICATION

This book is dedicated to
Lucy, Robin and Kate,
my three mythically lovely
and intelligent daughters.

INTRODUCTION

Glasgow urban myths, like that one about some Edinbuggers being occasionally pleasant, are as many and varied as Glaswegians themselves. There is the one about the well-to-do chap from the Mearns going into the city centre garage, after a hard day robbing punters, to pick up his Merc, and – shock, horror – it is gone. He reports it immediately to the police and they, of course, run him home promising immediate action. He is from the Mearns after all and forty years of rolling up your trouser leg has got to count for something.

Joy in the morning – the polis have found his car. It is where he left it, though it has definitely been taken away and returned. He goes down to the garage to check it out and finds a note on the dashboard saying: "Frightfully sorry, romantic emergency. I've filled the tank and I noticed a copy of *Opera Now* on your front seat so enclosed are a couple of tickets for the first night of *Don Giovanni* at the Theatre Royal next week. Apologies once again. I hope you enjoy the opera."

The mannie is chuffed to bits. He has got a good story for his golf club mates and a night out with the wife at one of his favourite operas, especially nice as it was written by a Mason. Off they go, have a pleasant wee pre-theatre supper, watch the Don get dragged off to hell and listen to *'Non mi dir, bell'idol mio'* from Donna Anna before heading back to their luxury detached bungalow.

Which has been completely stripped while they enjoyed the opera. The thieves had, thoughtfully, left the insurance documents on the kitchen table.

Then there is the one about the gay burglars, who break in, steal only your nicest bits of jewellery and rearrange the furniture so that it looks a lot better than it did. Or are they a myth?

Here you will find hard truths and blatant lies, albeit in a sort of hit-and-myth style, but you will laugh, and you will repeat them.

CHAPTER ONE

I was first told this story when I was working on the *Herald* Diary. I was phoned by a Glasgow City Councillor, who swore to me that it had happened to one of his constituents. No names, no pack drill, John, but that whisky that you promised if I didn't tell anyone that you believed it has been a long time in the post.

This bloke goes out on a Saturday night to a party and has a couple of beers. He meets a girl who seems to like him and she invites him to another party. She takes him to a flat in Ruchill and they continue to drink, and even get involved with some other recreational drugs. There may even be a bit of haughmagandie involved.

The next thing he knows, he wakes up, completely naked, in a bath filled with ice. He is still feeling the effects of the drugs and is totally hungover. He looks down at his chest, which has, "CALL 999 OR YOU WILL DIE" written on it in lipstick (good trick this, as it would need to be written upside down so that he could read it).

There is a phone on a stand next to the bath, so he picks it up and dials. He explains to the NHS 24 emergency operator, who is saying: "Are you really *sure* that this is life-threatening?" what the situation is and that he doesn't know where he is, what he has taken, or why he is really calling. She advises him to get out of the bath and look himself over in the mirror. He does, only to find two nine-inch slits in his lower back. She tells him to get back in the bath immediately, and they send an ambulance over. They find his kidneys have been removed. They are worth £10,000 each on the black market.

Who could possibly believe this absurd urban legend? But then again, it does provide the world with what it needs most – a new word, 'kidneynapping'. To the best of my knowledge, this has never happened. You need vast surgical teams to transfer kidneys, but, who knows, what with the march of technology, it may well become possible, and then the word will come into its own. And we will have 'organlegging' as well as, it occurs, 'footlegging'.

CHAPTER TWO

Threat to Italians from the Tartan Army:
Deep fry yer pizzas,
We're gonny deep fry yer pizzas.

And now one that everyone outside Scotland thinks is a myth. Deep-fried Mars bars are on sale right across Scotland, with more than a fifth of chip shops serving up the delicacy.

A study by NHS Greater Glasgow found 22% of Scottish takeaways had the foodstuff on its menu and another 17% used to sell them.

Researchers surveyed 500 chip shops and found children are the main buyers, with one shop selling up to 200 a week. The shops they interviewed also reported they have been asked to deep-fry Snickers, Creme Eggs and pizzas in the past.

Dr David Morrison, consultant in public health medicine, said, "We live in Scotland but we'd never actually seen deep-fried Mars bars for sale. We thought they might be fictitious. But the Scottish diet is a major health issue and it's important to know what the facts are. We can now confirm that there is no doubt – the deep-fried Mars bar is not just an urban myth."

Dr Morrison and his colleague Dr Mark Pettigrew decided to conduct the survey after the Mars bars received a mention on US television's *The Tonight Show* with Jay Leno on NBC. Their study is published in an issue of the medical journal *The Lancet*.

The Mars bar was first produced in 1920 by Frank and Ethel Mars in Tacoma, Washington, in the US. It was locally named the Milky Way but called the Mars bar in Europe and, as far as I can discover, has never been deep-fried in its country of origin. And who, on God's green earth, would want a larded-up Creme Egg?

I have tried, unsuccessfully, to convince an Italian woman of my acquaintance that in Scotland we deep-fry pizzas. "In lardo, no!" she says, and she will not believe me.

CHAPTER THREE

As they sing in Belarus:
Here we glow,
Here we glow,
Here we glow.

Of all the many monuments in the Southern Necropolis, one has gained a unique and mysterious reputation. It is the resting place of John S Smith, carpet manufacturer, his wife Magdalene and their housekeeper Mary McNaughton. In the form of a veiled woman beside a broken pillar, the ivy-covered and much-weathered memorial tells a fascinating story. Although the date of her husband's death is no longer visible on the stone, the tragic story behind the accidental death of Magdalene and her housekeeper is poignantly told.

On 29 October 1933, while returning to their home at Langside Avenue from church and sheltering from the heavy rain behind an umbrella, they walked into the path of a tramcar on Queen's Drive. Both were taken to the nearby Victoria Infirmary, but sadly Magdalene died on arrival and Mrs McNaughton passed away two weeks later. The monument is a solemn and fitting memorial to the tragedy. Local myth tells how the White Lady turns her head as you pass. Should she catch your eye, you will be turned to stone. There is, from personal knowledge, a mysterious glow about the White Lady at dead of night, or was that just me?

CHAPTER FOUR

This is the one where all the guys go:
"Oyaah!"

I heard this one a few years back. This is a story of a guy in Springburn who was a bit despondent over a recent fight with a girlfriend and decided he needed a little fresh air to clear his head. He thought he'd climb a pylon, of which, if you live in Springburn, you have a choice. He proceeded to climb his chosen pylon, but before doing so decided that a few beers might help his thinking on the subject.

So here he is, 60 feet up, drinking his beer, trying to soothe his bruised ego, as one does. He had five beers when he decided he needed the toilet, as you do after five beers. As it was such a long climb down, he decided to pee off the pylon.

Electricity is a funny thing. You don't need to touch a wire in order to get a shock. Depending on the conditions, you could be as far away as six feet and still get shocked.

The Special Brew kid proceeded to make water, almost certainly unaware that salt water is an excellent conductor of electricity, and the electricity arced up the stream, up to his wedding tackle, and blew him off the pylon.

The line went down and the lecky guys sent workmen to see if there was any damage. What they found was an extremely dead person, his fly down, a blackened smoking stump where his tackle had been, and a single Special Brew left on a girder of the pylon.

If this is actually true, please don't write in and tell me.

CHAPTER FIVE

This is the one that leaves
a bad taste in your mouth

This story was told to me by a friend of a friend of a friend who went on holiday to Spain with his family in their caravan. Being Glaswegian, they had not, of course, booked and, when they finally found a camp site that wasn't completely full, they discovered that they had to set up camp right next to a group of English football supporters. After a bit of harassment of their teenage daughters they complained to the management, but there was no room anywhere else, so they stayed in their caravan every day until the hooligans had left, but eventually lost patience after some late-night hassles and complained again.

The manager told the English guys to tone it down and threatened to evict them. The guys of course knew where the complaints were coming from, but seemed a bit intimidated, especially when one of them got nutted by another Scottish bloke on the site.

Then the family returned from a day trip to the village and saw some of these guys scurrying out of the caravan howling with laughter. They did not appear to be carrying anything that belonged to the family and they rushed to their caravan, only to find that nothing seemed to have been disturbed or taken. Cameras and other bits and pieces were still there.

Things seemed to settle down a bit after this and there was no more trouble, but when they got home and developed their holiday snaps they found photos of the English guys posing in the family's caravan with the family toothbrushes, bristle first, stuck up their bums.

CHAPTER SIX

Hardened criminal

This is possibly actually true, as a friend claims that he had a newspaper clipping of it that he carried round for years until it disintegrated.

A driver of a ready-mix concrete lorry left for his work one day in a bit of a hurry. Later in the morning he realized he had forgotten his sandwiches, so he decided to stop at his house during a delivery nearby and pick them up.

As he approached the house, he noticed a strange car outside. Curious, he entered quietly and tiptoed toward the bedroom, where he heard his wife and a strange male voice indulging in what was obviously a post-coital conversation.

Just as quietly, he left the house and walked to his lorry. He backed it up to the car and, poking the chute through a window that he quietly broke, filled the car with wet cement. He called his office on the mobile, confessed what he had done, and offered to pay for the concrete. Amid uproarious laughter, he was told that the load was on the company.

CHAPTER SEVEN

There is a moral to this story

This can't possibly be true – who would be that stupid? – but it's got enough legs to make people, especially engaged women, just a bit nervous.

A young couple were married in Glasgow Cathedral amid much joy and hoopla. The wedding was a large, elaborate festival – the bride was radiant and the groom handsome. Both families were delighted.

During the reception, the bride's father placed his dinner jacket on the back of his chair and went off to dance and socialize with his guests. Later in the evening, he looked into his jacket pocket for the three grand in cash he had brought to settle the bills with the band and several other people who had provided services. This gives it a wee ring of truth for me, as musos always want paid in cash. The money, of course, was gone, as was his wallet. What to do? His daughter's wedding couldn't end in disaster. Fortunately, one of his closest friends had a gold credit card. The guest paid all the bills, and the next day, the bride's father repaid him. But both were still astonished that a wedding guest had stolen the money.

A week later, the video photographer delivered the wedding video to the bride's family for checking before final edit. The father was amazed and a bit less than pleased to see footage of his new son-in-law removing his jacket from the chair and trousering the cash and wallet.

And the moral is, look for video cameras before you steal anything.

CHAPTER EIGHT

Getting ahead

I have been told that this is a genuine reply to a guy who had been pestering the Uni, but I don't believe it. It does have a kind of studenty feel to it, though, but the grammar is too good.

Paleoanthropology Department
Glasgow University.

Dear Sir,

Thank you for your latest submission to the University, labelled, "211-D, layer seven, next to the clothes pole. Hominid skull". We have given this specimen a careful and detailed examination, and regret to inform you that we disagree with your theory that it represents, "conclusive proof of the presence of Early Man in Priesthill two million years ago". It appears to us that what you have found is the head of a Barbie doll, of the variety one of our staff, who has small children, believes to be the "Wedding Barbie". It is evident that you have given a great deal of thought to the analysis of this specimen, and you may be quite certain that those of us who are familiar with your prior work in the field were loath to contradict your findings. However, we do feel that there are a number of physical attributes of the specimen which might have given you a clue or two to its modern origin:

1. The material is moulded plastic. Ancient hominid remains are usually fossilized bone. No, they are always fossilized bone. They are never, ever plastic. Really, not ever.

2. The cranial capacity of the specimen is approximately nine cubic centimetres, well below the threshold of even the earliest identified proto-hominids.

3. The dentition pattern evident on the "skull" is more consistent with the common domesticated scabby dug than it is with the "ravenous man-eating Pliocene whelks" that you speculate roamed the swamps of Scotland during that time. This latter finding is certainly one of the most intriguing hypotheses you have submitted in your history with this institution, but the evidence seems to weigh rather heavily

against it. Without going into too much detail, let us say that:

A. The specimen looks like the head of a Barbie doll that has been chewed by a dog.

B. Whelks don't have teeth.

It is with feelings tinged with melancholy that we must deny your request to have the specimen carbon dated. This is partially due to the heavy load our laboratory must bear in its normal operation, and partly due to carbon dating's notorious inaccuracy in fossils of recent geologic record. To the best of our knowledge, no Barbie dolls were produced prior to the 1950s, and carbon dating is likely to produce wildly inaccurate results.

Sadly, we must also deny your request that we approach the Phylogeny Department with the concept of assigning your specimen the scientific name, "Scottijockodus Gaunyadancer". Speaking personally, I, for one, fought tenaciously for the acceptance of your proposed taxonomy, but was ultimately voted down because the species name that you selected was stupid, and didn't really sound like it might be Latin.

However, we gladly accept your generous donation

of this fascinating specimen to the University. While it is undoubtedly not a hominid fossil, it is, nonetheless, yet another riveting example of the great body of work you seem to accumulate here so effortlessly. You should know that our Director has reserved a special shelf in his own office for the display of the specimens you have previously submitted to us, and the entire staff speculates daily on what you will happen upon next in your digs at the site you have discovered in your back green. We eagerly anticipate the trip to visit us that you proposed in your last letter, and several of us are pressing the Director to pay for it. We are particularly interested in hearing you expand on your theories of the "trans-positating fillifitation of ferrous ions in a structural matrix" that makes the excellent juvenile Tyrannosaurus Rex femur you recently discovered take on the deceptive appearance of a rusty 9mm shifting spanner.

Yours most sincerely,

Name withheld by request.

CHAPTER NINE

I'm going to join

Dear Friendly Wee Pal,

How many times have you wanted to fill that yawning spiritual void in your life but just weren't able to find the time or the energy? How often have you wanted to form a more personal relationship with a Higher Authority but just couldn't get turned on by that same old tired selection of Supreme Beings? Haven't you ever wished there was just one religion out there that understood you, Friendly Wee Pal, that indulged you, one that fitted in with your creative, dynamic lifestyle? Well, at last, thanks to the creators of Weegieism, there is. Finally, there's a faith that works for you, Friendly Wee Pal, instead of the other way around. After all these years, and following an in-depth market research study, Weegieists Worldwide (a non-profit agency not affiliated with anyone) has come up with a religion that draws upon the best features of some of the world's most popular denominations, but does them all far better.

Yes, Wee Pal, that's right! Weegieism is everything some religions are and much, much more. It's not just a job, it's an adventure; it's everything you always wanted in a God and less. Designed using the latest in CAR (Computer-Aided Religion) technology, here's just a few of the features Weegieism offers:

Guaranteed Salvation. Guaranteed.

Other religions require you to behave a certain way in the here-and-now in order to make it to the hereafter, but with Weegieism, you can do whatever you want, because your salvation is guaranteed! Weegieism realizes you've got enough to worry about in life without having to be nervous about where you're headed after you die, so relax! As a Weegieist, death means never having to have said you're sorry. Whatever heaven you want is yours, or, if you'd rather just be dead, that's fine, too.

Your Choice of Supreme Being.

No more arguing about who is more all-powerful Jesus or Mohammed, Buddha or Joe Smith. Stop fighting about whether Allah could beat the Holy Ghost in a wrestling match. End the endless bickering over whether the Supreme Deity is a He or a She. With Weegieism, you can choose. Using the patented Godolyzer, you make God in your image. Combine Jesus' hairdo with Mother Nature's eyes. Add the musical flair of Krishna to the sexual swagger of Zoroaster. You want a Lord who's vengeful but also knows how to rock? No problem. Using the Godolyzer, with or without the templates provided, it's *your* choice.

Eat Whatever You Want.

Remember fish on Friday? Or how about unleavened bread? Kosher, who needs it? As a Weegieist, you'll never have to tongue another eucharist wafer off your palate or nurse another hangover brought on from sacramental wine again. Glut your gums however you'd like, whenever you'd like. Take all you want, just want all you take.

More Efficient Commandments.

Some religions take as many as ten Commandments to lay down their laws. Weegieism, using the latest in data-compression techniques, has significantly reduced the number of Commandments and has also managed to dramatically decrease their stringency. Think of them simply as a Couple of Suggestions, and if you'd rather not, hey, Wee Pal, that's quite all right, too.

No Sexual Taboos.

Has anything turned more people away from the power above the heavens than the power below their waists? Weegieism doesn't have this problem because, as a Weegieist you, Friendly Wee Pal, can stick or get stuck however you want with whom or whatever you want whenever or wherever you want. As long as no one gets hurt – or just if they want to – Weegieism says have fun. And be safe.

More and Better Holidays.

Even the most fun-loving religions usually have only half a dozen or so major holidays a year. And often several of these are days of atonement or fasting. Weegieism, on the other hand, features a full complement of 365 full-scale religious holidays a year! 366 for a leap year. And all include presents and feasting.

No Stupid and Dangerous Joining Rituals.

No hitting with sticks. No drenchings in water. No knives aimed at your privates. No bits hacked off your penis. No rolling up of your trouser leg. Need we say more?

No Annual Fee.

Because of low overheads (no Gothic cathedrals

to keep up, no sacred texts to maintain, no Crusades to mount) Weegieism is offered to you entirely free! A letter now and again would be nice, but hey, don't worry about it.

100% Compatibility.

Weegieism does not require you to change or upgrade any of your existing religious or sectarian beliefs. It is in no way mutually exclusive. You can be a Weegieist and anything else you want too, even a Tory.

Leave at Any Time.

No forms to fill out. No one will phone you. You can be a Weegieist one day and something else the next. Change hourly if you'd like. By the second if you'd prefer. Or, be a Weegieist forever. It's entirely up to you. So, there you have it, Wee Pal, in a nutshell – a pistachio to be exact. With Weegieism, you get all the plusses of other religions with none of the minuses. It's like having your cake and eating it, too. It is, in fact, like owning the whole baker's shop. And because you, Friendly Wee Pal, are who you are, and only sometimes somebody else, you have been selected to participate in this charter membership offer. As a Weegieist, you'll enjoy the benefits of the world's only computer-designed faith as well as the peace of mind of knowing that if Armageddon does come, it's not your fault!

So join today and start receiving the benefits immediately. All you have to do is whatever you want. Make no phone calls unless you feel so inclined. Write no letters unless it strikes your fancy. Send no money, unless you want to.

Be a Weegieist or don't be. You are still surrounded in a warm cone-shaped cocoon of love.

Very sincerely, or perhaps not,

Snakehips McGunnagle

P.S. This offer never expires. Relax and breathe deeply.

The above is obviously nonsense. I know Snakehips, and he is an atheist.

CHAPTER TEN

The Nae Luck of Any Kind Awards, and penguins

Following an intense forest fire that burned several hundred acres, firemen were surprised to find a diver, in full wetsuit, fins, mask and tanks, hanging dead from the charred remains of a tree. Investigators were stumped (like many of the trees) at first but eventually came up with a unique theory.

The Scottish Fire Brigades recently began using a helicopter with a drogue that can scoop up large volumes of water from the sea or a loch, fly to the scene of a fire, dump its contents and quickly put out a fire.

Thus the theory is that the diver was scooped up by the plane and dropped over the fire.

A bricklayer working on a three-storey tall chimney had set up a pulley system so that his hod man could raise the bricks up to where he needed them. As he was working, his helper was complaining about how difficult it would be to get the last of the bricks up to the flat roof of the building. Just then, another contractor had some material delivered and it was placed on the roof by a forklift brought to unload it. The bricklayer asked if the driver would load his bricks up there as well, and for a fiver the driver agreed. The brickie realized that he would not need his mate any more and sent him home.

As the bricklayer completed the chimney he noticed that he had quite a few bricks left over and that the forklift was no longer at the site. Now he had to work out how to get the spare bricks back down by himself. If you drop bricks from that height, they break, and it is dangerous. So he decided to use the pulley that he had set up to lower them down.

First he went down to the ground and raised a large metal bucket up to the roof level using the rope and pulley. Next, he tied the rope off on to a railing, climbed back up to the roof and loaded the bricks into the bucket. Then he went back down to the ground.

He knew that the bricks would be heavy, so he wrapped the rope around his hand a couple of times and then untied the end of the rope with his other hand. The bricks were just that wee bit heavier than he had imagined and, with the laws of physics being what they are, he was immediately launched upwards at a high rate of knots.

As he was racing up towards the roof he encountered the bucket full of bricks coming down at an equally fast rate.

He collided with the bucket and broke his nose and his shoulder. The bucket passed him by as he sped upwards. He reached the pulley just before the bucket hit the ground and broke three of his fingers as they were pulled into the pulley. When the bucket hit the ground, it tipped and the bricks spilled on to the ground.

Close your eyes and visualise the scene. As the now light bucket sped upwards, the mason took an eye-watering dunt in the groin when one of his legs slipped into the empty bucket.

He then tilted enough to fall out of the bucket and continued with his gravity experiment. Eventually he landed on top of the pile of bricks and broke a leg. He collapsed in pain there on the bricks, but was glad to be alive, so he let go of the rope and cried out for help. Very shortly afterwards the bucket, still obeying the laws of physics, fractured his skull.

An acquaintance of mine who was a contractor there told me that bored Royal Air Force pilots stationed on the Falkland Islands have devised what they consider a marvellous new game. Noting that the local penguins are fascinated by aeroplanes, the pilots search out a beach where the birds are gathered and fly slowly along it at the water's edge. Perhaps ten thousand penguins turn their heads in unison watching the planes go by, and when the pilots turn around and fly back, the birds turn their heads in the opposite direction, like spectators at a slow-motion tennis match. Then, he says, "The pilots fly out to sea and then directly to the penguin colony and fly slowly over it. Heads go up, up, up, and ten thousand penguins fall over gently on to their backs."

Then of course they have to p-p-p-p-pick themselves up.

CHAPTER ELEVEN

Two loads of fanny

Subject: Internet Clean-Up Day
THIS MESSAGE WILL BE REPEATED
IN MID-FEBRUARY.
*** Attention ***

It's that time again!

As many of you know, each year the Internet in Scotland must be shut down for 24 hours in order to allow us to clean it and give it a wee tidy. The cleaning process, which eliminates dead email and inactive FTP, www etc, means we get a better working and faster Internet.

This year, the cleaning process will take place from 12:01 a.m. GMT on February 27 until 12:01 a.m. GMT on February 28 (the time least likely to interfere with ongoing work). During that 24-hour period, five powerful Internet search engines situated around Scotland will search the Internet and delete any data that they find.

In order to protect your valuable data from

deletion we ask that you do the following:

1. Disconnect all terminals and local area networks from their Internet connections.

2. Shut down all Internet servers, or disconnect them from the Internet.

3. Disconnect all disks and hard drives from any connections to the Internet.

4. Refrain from connecting any computer to the Internet in any way.

We understand the inconvenience that this may cause some Internet users, and we apologize. However, we are certain that any inconveniences will be more than made up for by the increased speed and efficiency of the Internet once it has been cleared of electronic flotsam and jetsam.

We thank you for your cooperation.

The above is complete nonsense, but there have been versions of it around for years. This is the first specifically Scottish one I've seen. "A wee tidy", indeed. Delete it if you get it and don't forward it.

A young friend of my daughter's was due a gynae check and was a bit nervous, so she cleaned up and scooshed herself from the wee plastic bottle to make herself smell nice. When she gets to the clinic and she's in the stirrups, the doctor comments: "Aye, very nice." The young woman was mortified and completely embarrassed that the doctor would comment in this way, and was thinking of making a complaint.

When she arrived home and went to the loo, she discovered that she had used glitter spray and not deodorant.

CHAPTER TWELVE

Rats and scary stories

Someone repeated this next one to me recently as happening to his sister's boyfriend. I seem to remember that it started life as a Jim Kelman short story, years ago, or maybe Jim was just passing it on.

A young guy in a supermarket in Glasgow was sent to clean up a store room. When he got back, he was complaining that it was really filthy and that he had noticed dried mouse or rat droppings in some areas.

A couple of days later, he started feeling that he was coming down with the flu, aching joints, headache, etc, and he started throwing up. He went to bed and never really got up. Within two days his face and eyeballs were yellow. He was rushed to emergency at the Western, where they said he was suffering from organ failure. He died shortly before midnight.

The doctors specifically asked if he had been in a warehouse or exposed to dried rat or mouse droppings at any time. They said there is a virus that lives in dried rat and mouse droppings. A post-mortem was conducted to verify the doctors' suspicions. This is why it is extremely important to *always* carefully rinse off the tops of any cans of soft drinks or foods.

There is a whole lot more of this nonsense, and it *is* nonsense. Always a good idea to wash the top of a can, though.

I know a lot of rumours have been going around about planned or possibly planned terrorist attacks. Most of these emails I read and just go on about my day. This, however, sounds *serious*.

Don't go to the toilet on October 19th. The CID reports that a major plot is planned for that day. Anyone who has a jobbie on the 19th will be bitten on the bum by a big black dog. Reports indicate that organized groups of dogs are planning to rise up into unsuspecting Glaswegians' toilet bowls and bite them when they are going about their business.

I usually don't send emails like this, but I got this information from a reliable source. It came from a friend of a friend whose cousin is going out with this girl whose brother knows this guy whose wife knows this woman whose husband buys smuggled fags from this guy who knows a shoe shop man who sells shoes to a postal worker who has a friend who's a drug dealer who sells drugs to another man who works for the government. He apparently overheard two men talking in the toilet about big black dogs and came to the conclusion that we are going to be attacked.

So it must be true.

You know how I know it isn't true? Men don't talk in toilets.

CHAPTER THIRTEEN

Unlucky for some

The ultimate myth and hoax email.

The following was forwarded to me and it is absolutely true. Everyone knows that I don't send out erroneous emails. This completely clears up all the misunderstandings concerning internet hoaxes, conspiracy theories, pranks, schemes etc. Of course, the following information has been confirmed by the CID and/or the government. So next time you are unsure if an email that you have received is true or not, please check with the following to confirm its accuracy. If you feel that any particular hoax or theory has been left out, please email it to me with the details and I will include it in future. Once again, the following is 100% true and well worth the read.

The children's tattoos laced with LSD that were supposed to be used for satanic ritual abuse at that nursery in Possil were mistakenly eaten by the choking Dobermann who was bitten by the snake that came out of the fur coat that was worn by the escaped homicidal maniac whose hook was found hanging from the door of the car of the teenagers who ran out of a lover's lane when they heard that he had escaped and then went to the dope party where the girls who were supposed to be babysitting got wasted on dope and were so stoned they accidentally put the baby in the oven because the microwave was ruined by the exploding poodle that the girl with the beehive hairdo that turned out to contain beetles who had got an automatic First at college because her friend had committed suicide had put in to dry after it had got wet chasing the vanishing hitchhiker who had tried to warn the girl that her insides were cooked because she had stayed too long under the sun lamp at the local skin cancer inducer while her dad won a contest at that radio channel that played rock records that contained hidden commands and subliminal messages planted by the Jews, the Muslims, international bankers, the Illuminati, multinational corporations, and the spooks at Hanger 18 of Area 51 in Dreamland who performed the autopsies on the aliens who crashed at Roswell, New Mexico while on a mission to abduct people and conduct weird sexual and reproductive experiments on them because they knew we use only ten percent of our brains and that engineers had "proved" that bumblebees can't fly and that sugar wakes you up even if you're an MI5 agent who has recovered memories about conspiring with criminals and anti-New Labour extremists who woke up after a one-night stand in a hotel only to find that the girl he was with was gone and had written "Welcome to the world of Aids" in lipstick on the bathroom mirror which terrified him because he knew that it is just as easy to get Aids from heterosexual intercourse as it is from homosexual sodomy with an IV drug user because when the US government created Aids to commit genocide against black people who aren't adversely affected by the minimum wage with the aid of immigrants who don't give anything back to the community while smoking a cigarette that has no more been proven to give you cancer than evolution has been proven to occur because it's only a theory and there are no real fossils and it violates the second law of thermodynamics unlike creation science which is not religious and fear of irradiated food which is rational because we know the government can improve our lives by suspending the laws of supply and demand to make prices fair and deciding how many people of each race and sex should be in universities and jobs which is good, because when control of everyday life is centralized in the New Labour-controlled state the people who make the decisions are never capricious or high-handed or make decisions favouring their friends and family and people who pay them money because if only we can get the right people into positions of control it will be safe to let them run things because clever people can work out how to allocate resources and what fair prices are for goods and services and work and who should be allowed to do what much more efficiently and constructively than just letting millions of people make their own decisions about what they should eat or drink or smoke or for whom they should work for under what conditions for how much money on what schedule based on their own perceptions, concerns and plans in accordance with their best interests.

But I digress.

CHAPTER FOURTEEN

A Craigton tale

A group of teenage girls were having a party one night when one of them had an empty (parents away for the weekend) and began to exchange ghost stories. One girl claimed that the old man who had been buried earlier that week in the cemetery at the back of the scheme had been buried alive. She claimed that, if you tried, you could hear him still scratching at the lid of his coffin. The other girls called her bluff and told her that she wouldn't do it. They said she was too afraid to go down to the grave that very night. They continued to challenge her and eventually she gave in and accepted their challenge. Since she was going to go alone, she needed to prove to the others that she actually followed through with the task. She was supposed to take a wooden stake with her (presumably also useful against vampires) and drive it into the ground so the next day the girls would know that she had been to the grave.

She headed off, stake in hand, and never returned. The other girls assumed she had chickened out and had just gone home ashamed.

The next morning as they passed the cemetery they saw her there at the old man's grave. Kneeling in the dark she had accidentally staked her dressing gown to the ground and when she tried to move away from the grave and felt the tugging, she died of fright.

CHAPTER FIFTEEN

Abominable a bomb in a bull story
and a little old lady. Bless.

A worker at one of the big dairy farms who heard that bovine flatulence was largely composed of methane, and potentially explosive, decided to apply the scientific method to the theory.

While one of his contented cow charges was hooked up to the milking machine, he waited for the slight tail lift which dairy workers know signals an impending expulsion, generally something to avoid. Our hero flicked his lighter. His satisfaction at seeing the resulting foot-long blue flame lasted mere seconds, before the flame was subsumed by a rectal contraction. The poor cow exploded, killing the worker, who was struck by a flying femur.

And here is a letter from a South Side retirement home.

Dear Schoolchildren,

Thank you so much for the beautiful radio I won at your recent pensioners' bingo lunch. I'm 94 years old and live at the local home in Pollokshields. My family are all dead apart from my daughter in Australia and I rarely have visitors. As a result, I have very limited contact with the outside world. This makes your present especially welcome.

The woman who shares my room, Maggie Cook, has had her own radio for as long as I've known her. She listens to it all the time, though usually with an earplug or with the volume so low that I can't hear it. For some reason I have never understood, she has never wanted to share it.

Last Sunday morning, while listening to her morning religious programme, she accidentally knocked her radio off its shelf. It smashed into many pieces, and caused her to cry. It was really sad.

Fortunately, I had my new radio. Knowing this, Maggie asked if she could listen to mine.

I told her to fuck off.

God bless you.

CHAPTER SIXTEEN

Phone phantasy. With eejits.

I was sitting at my desk, when I remembered a phone call I had to make. I found the number and rang it. A man answered saying, "Hello?" I politely said, "This is John Thomas. Could I please speak to Robin Carter?"

Without a word the phone was slammed down on me. I couldn't believe that anyone could be that rude. I tracked down Robin's correct number and rang her. She had transposed the last two digits in her email. After I finished talking to Robin, I spotted the wrong number still lying there on my desk and decided to call it again.

When the same person once more answered, I shouted "Fuckin' eejit!" and hung up. Next to his phone number I wrote the word "Eejit," and put it in my desk drawer. Every couple of weeks, when I was feeling rotten, or had had a really bad day, I'd phone him. He'd answer, and then I'd yell, 'Fuckin' eejit!" It would always cheer me up.

Later that year BT introduced caller ID. This was

a real disappointment for me. I would have to stop calling the eejit. Then one day I had an idea. I rang his number, then heard his voice, "Hello," I made up a name, "this is Peter Smith with BT. I'm just calling to see if you're familiar with our caller ID offer?" He went "No!", and slammed the phone down. I quickly called him back and said, "That's because you're a fuckin' eejit!"

And the reason I took the time to tell you this story is to show you how if there's ever anything really bothering you, you can do something about it. Just ring 0141 429 7987.

The wee old woman at the supermarket took her time pulling out of the parking space. I didn't think she was ever going to leave. Finally her car began to move and she started to very slowly back out of the space. I backed up a little more to give her plenty of room to pull out.

All of a sudden this black BMW comes flying up in the wrong direction and pulls into the space I have been more or less patiently waiting for. I honked my horn and shouted, but the guy climbed out of his car completely ignoring me. He walked toward the supermarket doors as if he didn't even hear me. I thought to myself, this guy's a fuckin' eejit.

I noticed he had a 'For Sale' sign in the back window of his car. I wrote down the number and found another place to park.

A couple of days later, I'm at home sitting at my desk. I had just got off the phone after ringing the number above and yelling, "Fuckin' eejit!" (It's really easy to phone him now since I have his number on speed dial.) I noticed the phone number of the man with the black Beamer lying on my desk and thought I'd ring him too.

After a couple of rings someone answered the phone and said, "Hello." I said, "You the chap with the black BMW for sale?"

"Yes I am."

"Can you tell me where I can see it?"

"Yes, I live in Bearsden, 17 Glasgow Road. It's a yellow house and the car's parked outside."

I said, "What's your name?"

"My name is Julian Dawson."

"When's a good time to catch you, Julian?"

"I'm at home most evenings."

"Listen, Julian, can I tell you something?"

"Yes."

"Julian, you're a fuckin' eejit!" And I slammed the phone down. After I hung up I added his number to my speed dialler.

For a while things seemed to be going better for me. Now when I had a problem I had two eejits to call. Then after several months of phoning the eejits and hanging up on them, the whole thing started to seem like an obligation. It just wasn't as enjoyable as it used to be. I gave the problem some serious thought and came up with a solution.

First, I rang Eejit no.1.

A man answered, "Hello."

I yelled "Fuckin' eejit!" But I didn't hang up.

The eejit said, "Are you still there?"

I said, "Yes."

He said, "Stop phoning me."

I said, "No."

He said, "What's your fuckin' name, pal?"

I said, "Julian Dawson."

"Where do you live?"

Bearsden, 17 Glasgow Road. It's a yellow house and my black BMW is parked out front."

"I'm coming over right now."

"Yeah, like I'm really feart. Fuckin' eejit!" and I hung up.

Then I called Eejit no.2.

He answered, "Hello."

I said, "Hello? Fuckin' eejit!"

He said, "If I ever find out who you are . . ."

"You'll what?"

"I'll kick your fuckin' arse!"

"Oh aye? You just wait right there. I'm coming over right now, eejit!"

Then I hung up.

Anybody notice an affray or some bad behaviour in Glasgow Road last July?

Maggie Stewart of Glasgow had a serious telephone problem. But, unlike most people, she did something about it.

The brand-new £10 million Bideawee Deluxe Hotel opened nearby and had acquired almost the same telephone number as Maggie.

From the moment the hotel opened, Maggie was besieged by calls not for her. Since she had had the same phone number for years, she felt that she had a case to persuade the hotel management to change its number.

Naturally, the management refused, claiming that it could not change its stationery.

BT weren't helpful, either. A number was a number was a number, and just because a customer was getting someone else's calls 24 hours a day didn't make it responsible. After her plea fell on deaf ears, Maggie decided to take matters into her own hands. At 9 o'clock the phone rang. Someone from Glasgow was calling the hotel and asked for a room for the following Tuesday. Maggie said, "No bother. How many nights?"

A few hours later Edinburgh was on. A secretary

wanted a suite with two bedrooms for a week. Emboldened, Maggie said the Sheridan Suite was available for £600 a night. The secretary said that she would take it and asked if the hotel wanted a deposit. "No, that won't be necessary," Maggie said. "We trust you."

The next day was a busy one for Maggie. In the morning, she booked two funeral purveys and a 21st, but her biggest challenge came in the afternoon when a mother called to book the ballroom for her daughter's wedding in June.

Maggie assured the woman that it would be no problem and asked if she would be providing the flowers or did she want the hotel to take care of it. The mother said that she would prefer the hotel to handle the floral arrangements. Oh joy.

Within a few weeks, the Bideawee Deluxe was a nightmare. People kept showing up for rooms, weddings, funerals, and school reunion parties and were all told there were no such events.

Maggie had her final revenge when she read in the *Herald*'s Business section that the hotel might go bankrupt. Her phone rang, and an executive from Stakis said, "We're prepared to offer you £200,000 for the hotel."

Maggie replied. "We'll take it, but only if you change the telephone number."

CHAPTER SEVENTEEN

A young man from Glasgow who wants his Mammy and is a wee bit slow, and an older man who is pretty quick.

A young man is shopping in a Glasgow supermarket when he notices that an older woman seems to be following him, staring at him in a sorrowful manner. He moves to the next aisle, trying to avoid her, but she follows, still staring.

And when he finishes shopping, he ends up behind her in a long queue. Her trolley is overflowing; his contains just a few items.

She keeps staring at him sadly, making him feel a bit freaked. Finally she speaks up. "I'm sorry about staring," she says, "but you look exactly like my son, who died just two weeks ago." And she begins to sniffle. "I mean, exactly like him," she whispers.

Then, as the checkout girl processes her groceries, the woman asks: "As a favour to a grief-stricken mother, would you mind saying 'Cheerio, Mammy' to me as I leave? Somehow, it would make me feel so much better."

The young guy gulps and agrees to her request. She gives him a tearful smile, waves, and walks quickly towards the car park with her head down.

"Cheerio, Mammy!" he says, waving back.

All the scene needs now to make it a perfect melodrama is violins welling up in the background, or maybe a little supermarket muzak.

The young man, reflecting on his good deed, feels such a warm glow of self-satisfaction that he barely notices the girl ringing up his own few purchases. Until, that is, the cashier tells him that the bill comes to £110.43.

"There must be a mistake," the young man says, pointing at his single small bag.

The girl said, "Your mother said you'd be paying for hers too."

Peter was back in Glasgow on a business trip and, after being out for dinner one evening, he decided to travel back to his hotel on the subway. He was just settling into his seat when he realised that his Rolex watch was missing.

On the platform stood a young man who was grinning at him and, reckoning that this was the thief, Peter leapt up and tried to get off the tube before the doors closed.

Unfortunately, he did not quite make it. Nevertheless, he managed to grab hold of the man's lapels only to rip them clean off his suit as the subway moved away, and also managed to whang the no longer grinning young guy off the end of the tunnel as the subway car reached it. When he got back to his hotel the first thing he did was to phone the police and report the theft. Then he phoned his wife to tell her of the loss and what had happened.

"Jesus," she said: "have you told anyone?" He said that he had been in touch with the polis. "Oh shit," she said, "you left your watch behind on the dresser this morning."

A couple returned early from a night out to find their teenage daughter having sex with her boyfriend on the couch. After the particularly awkward moments passed and the lad went home, the woman sat her daughter down for a "wee chat". She got to the part about using protection and the girl said: "Don't worry mum, I've been taking your birth control pills." The woman asked her why she'd never noticed any missing and the daughter said, "I replace them with those wee aspirin Dad takes for his heart."

CHAPTER EIGHTEEN

More bad taste, including a drunk driver

A bungling thief tried to siphon diesel from a camper van but got a mouthful of raw sewage. The would-be raider missed the fuel tank in the dark and put a tube into the van's septic tank by mistake. And after sucking up the foul-smelling waste, he threw up on the spot and fled.

Pensioner John O'Hare found a puddle of vomit and an abandoned petrol container when he stepped out of the van in the morning. And last night he smiled: "I hope the thief has learned from his experience and given up his evil ways."

John, 73, and wife May, 69, of Arden, Glasgow had spent a week touring Scotland before stopping off for the final night of their holiday in Helensburgh.

John said: "We made sure everything was safe and secure and settled down for the night. The following morning we were disgusted to find that under the cover of darkness a thief had attempted to siphon off diesel from the fuel tank. But fortunately for us, he was left with a nasty taste in his mouth."

John found a plastic siphon tube and an empty fuel container next to their camper.

The contents of the septic tank had been drained and lay on the ground next to a pool of the thief's vomit. Also abandoned at the scene was a pile of pound coins which John believes may have been stolen from a vending machine earlier in the night.

John and May donated the abandoned pound coins to Oxfam.

John said: "We hope this thief will give up robbing visitors and tourists seeking a peaceful and pleasant holiday after what happened to him."

"Given up his evil ways." Some Glasgow punter said that? Aye, right. The above story appeared in one of our Glasgow-based red tops a couple of years ago. Apart from the names, which one presumes are real, this story has been on the go for at least twenty years. And how did the pound coins jump out of his pocket on to the ground? Never believe everything that you read in the papers.

A junkie was in desperate need of a fix. He was willing to do anything, including breaking into the house of an old woman whose son was a dealer. That night the junkie approached the house with a brick, planning on smashing in a window. To his amazement, the door was unlocked. He walked in, unaware that her funeral had been that day, and in no time found what he thought was the cocaine on the mantelpiece. The next morning, the son came home to find his mother's cremation urn opened and the junkie asleep on the floor, with dusty remains on his shirt and face.

Joe goes to a party and has too much to drink. His friends plead with him to let them take him home. He says he only lives a mile away, in Milngavie. About five seconds after he has left the party the police pull him up, as he is all over the road, and ask him to get out of the car to be breathalysed. Just as he starts, the police radio blares out a notice of a burglary taking place in a house just a few yards down the street. The police tell Joe to stay where he is, they will be right back, and run down the street to the robbery.

Joe waits and waits for what seems ages and finally decides to drive home, which he does steadily, the shock of being nicked having sobered him up a tiny bit, though he is still totally banjaxed. When he gets there, he tells his wife he is going to bed, and to tell anyone who might come looking for him that he has got the flu and has been in bed all day.

Twenty minutes later the police knock on the door. They ask if Joe is there and his wife says yes. They ask to see him and she replies that he is in bed with the flu and has been so all day. The police have his licence. They ask to see his car and she asks why. They insist on seeing his car, so she takes them to the garage. She opens the door. There sitting in the garage, with all its lights still flashing, is the police car.

CHAPTER NINETEEN

Think you're smart, pal?

At Glasgow University during an examination one day, a bright young history student laid down his pen and asked his examiner to bring him a stoup of red wine.

Examiner: "Eh?"

Student: "I formally request that you bring me a stoup of red wine."

Examiner: "Sorry, laddie, no red or any other coloured wine for you."

Student: "Seriously, I really must insist. I request and require that you bring me a stoup of red wine."

At this point, the student produced a copy of the foundation document of 1451, written partially in Latin and still nominally in effect, and pointed to the section which read (rough translation from the Latin): "Gentlemen sitting examinations may request and require a stoup of red wine."

The examiners hemmed and hawed, and no one had any idea how much a stoup held, but nobody was getting on with their exams, and he said he would settle for a large glass of red wine. The exam recommenced, he was supplied with his stoup, and sat smugly slurping away, a minor master of beating the system.

The following day the university authorities fined him five Scots pounds for not wearing a sword. And nobody knew how much that was either.

A Glasgow gangster, Paddy Maguire, blags a considerable sum from his employers and takes off for the Costa del Plenty, where he goes to ground. No one can find him. This is because he is dead, and the going to ground is literal, as in into the ground. Do not steal from Glasgow gangsters.

He has, however, left a large chunk of this loot with his ever-loving wife, who is freaked out by the event and scared at the amount of the money. In her paranoia she spends huge amounts on security. No other house in Glasgow has this level of burglar and assault-proofedness. The gravel on the path is electrified. There are radars, sonars, automatic machine guns, landmines, guards. There are alarms on the alarms. This house is better protected than the Crown jewels.

She comes down one morning to find a car in her living room, not a big one, just one of the new

Volkswagens, but there is no sign of any kind as to how it got there. The doors of the room are normal sized, no alarms have rung. She opens the door of the car and finds a letter, nicely handwritten, on the dashboard. It says: "Mrs Maguire, when we want our money back, we'll ask for it."

CHAPTER TWENTY

A couple of bum notes and a bad joke

A Glasgow couple are up in Glenshee, with a group of friends, giving it laldy on the ski slopes. Conditions are just about perfect, wind whistling, cold as a witch's tit, no feeling in the toes, basic numbness all over. All in all, a "Tell me when we're having a good time" kind of day.

The woman complained to her husband that she was in dire need of a toilet, as the cold was getting to her. He told her not to worry, that he was sure there was relief waiting at the top of the lift in the form of a loo for female skiers in distress. He was wrong, of course, and the pain did not go away. Leg-crossing was losing its effect.

When you hear the siren call of nature going "Now! Now! Now!" you know that a temperature of below zero doesn't help matters. So, with time running out, the woman weighed up her options.

Her husband, picking up on the intensity of the pain, suggested that since she was wearing an all-white ski outfit, she should go off behind a tree. No one would even notice, he assured her. The white will provide more than adequate camouflage. So she headed for the trees, disrobed and proceeded to do her thing. If you've ever parked on the side of a slope, then you know there is a right way and wrong way to set up your skis so you don't move. Yep, you got it. She had them positioned the wrong way.

Steep slopes are not forgiving, even during embarrassing moments. Without warning, the woman found herself skiing backwards, out of control, racing through the trees, somehow missing all of them, and into another slope. Her bum and the rest were still bare, her salopettes and knickers down around her knees, and she was picking up speed all the while.

She continued proceeding in a backward direction, creating an unusual vista for the other skiers. The poor woman skied, if you define that verb loosely, back under the lift and finally collided violently with a pylon. The bad news was that she broke her arm and was unable to pull up her trousers. When her husband finally arrived, and put an end to her nude show, they called staff and an ambulance, which transported her to hospital.

In the ward after the painkillers she was getting her head together when a man with an obviously broken leg was put in the bed next to hers.

"How did you break your leg?" she asked.

"It was the weirdest thing I've ever seen," he said. "I was riding up in the ski lift, and suddenly I couldn't believe my eyes. There was this mad woman skiing backward down the slope with her bare bum hanging out and her trousers down around her knees.

"I leaned over to get a better look and I just didn't realize how far I'd moved. I fell out of the lift. How did you break your arm?"

At her wedding reception in a Glasgow hotel a bride decided to play a joke on her new husband. He was a devoted follower of the lottery and stuck to the same numbers every week, so she handed a copy of his numbers to the DJ and asked him to read them out at a certain point in the evening.

At the allotted time, the DJ paused the celebrations to announce the winning lottery numbers. The husband as normal checked his lottery ticket, and with loud shouts of joy raced to the bar and ordered the bar staff to serve free champagne all round.

Alarmed at the speed her husband and the guests were drinking, the bride asked her husband to join her on stage for an announcement. The husband leapt on stage, grabbed the mike and started to make a speech.

"I would like to thank you all for being here to celebrate this wondrous occasion where I have been so blessed – not once but twice". Turning to his new wife and clutching his lottery ticket he said: "I have something to confess to you – for the past six months I have been having an affair with your sister and we are leaving together tonight."

It was left to the DJ to explain the joke to the husband after the wife had collapsed on stage.

A Bearsden man was working on his motorbike on the patio and his wife was in the house in the kitchen. The man was racing the engine on the bike and somehow it slipped into gear. The man, still holding the handlebars, was dragged through a glass patio door and the motorbike dumped on the floor inside the house. The wife, hearing the crash, ran into the room and found her husband lying on the floor, cut and bleeding, the motorcycle lying next to him and the patio door shattered. The wife ran to the phone and summoned an ambulance. Because they lived on a fairly large hill, the wife went down the several flights of long steps to the street to direct the paramedics to her husband.

After the ambulance arrived and transported the husband to the hospital, the wife righted the motorcycle and pushed it outside. Seeing that petrol had spilled on the floor, the wife got some paper towels and blotted up the petrol.

The husband was treated at the hospital and was released to come home. When he got back he looked at the shattered patio door and the damage done to his bike. He became depressed and thought he'd cheer himself up with a smoke. He went into the bathroom, sat on the loo and smoked a cigarette. After finishing the cigarette, he flipped it between his legs into the toilet bowl while still seated. The wife, who was in the kitchen, heard a loud explosion and her husband screaming. She had of course thrown the petrol-soaked paper towels in the toilet.

She broke into the bathroom and found her husband lying on the floor. His trousers had been blown away and he was suffering burns on the buttocks, the back of his legs and his groin. The wife again ran to the phone and called for an ambulance. The same ambulance crew was dispatched and the wife met them at the street. The paramedics loaded the husband on to the stretcher and began carrying him to the street.

While they were going down the stairs to the street accompanied by the wife, one of the paramedics asked the wife how the husband had burned himself. She told them and the paramedics started laughing so hard, one of them tipped the stretcher and dumped the husband out. He fell down the remaining steps and broke his ankle.

He got a very nice new bike out of the damages.

CHAPTER TWENTY-ONE

Not so daft,
and you must be choking, surely

A young woman was driving alone one night near the local asylum when she heard on the radio that a dangerous man had escaped. Within minutes she heard a pop and felt one of her tyres go flat. Her moby had run out of juice, so she got herself together, built up her nerve and got out and began to change the tyre. Just as she slid the spare wheel on she noticed a man in a plain white uniform staring at her from the bushes. Startled, she dropped the wheel nuts and heard them scatter on the ground. As she vainly searched in the darkness for the scattered nuts she heard the man slowly approaching. Terrified, she asked herself in a trembling voice: "What am I going to do now?" and the patient replied, "Why don't you take one nut from each of the other wheels and put them on the spare?" She did, and was soon on her way.

A woman from Bearsden saw a blind man picking his way through a crowd and went over to help. The two started to talk and the man asked her if she could deliver the letter he held in his hand to the address on the envelope. She was passing that address on the way home anyway, so she agreed.

She started out to deliver the message, when she turned around to see if there was anything else the blind man needed. But she spotted him hurrying through the crowd without his dark glasses or white cane. She went to the police, who raided the address on the envelope, where they found organs, limbs and entire bodies, a veritable charnel house.

The women opened the envelope to see what it said, and it was:

"This is the last one I am sending you today."

A Drumchapel woman came home from shopping up the toon to find her Dobermann choking on something. She quickly put him in the car and drove him to the vet. The vet told her to go home while he operated to remove whatever was lodged in the dog's windpipe and he'd ring to tell her when she could pick up her pet. She wasn't home for long when the vet called and told her in an excited voice to get out of the house *right now* and he'd be there to explain in a few minutes. From her neighbour's window she saw the vet arrive with the police and ran out to see if her dog was all right and what was going on. As the police ran into her house the vet told her what her loving pet had choked on, two human fingers. The police found an escaped murderer hiding in the hall cupboard nursing his mangled hand.

CHAPTER TWENTY-TWO

Some things that people in my pub
have sworn to me are true.
Some of them believe all of these.

Cabbage Patch kids were modelled after mentally defective children to get people used to what children would look like after a nuclear war.

If you yelled for 8 years, 7 months and 6 days you would have produced enough sound energy to heat one cup of tea.

If you farted consistently for 6 years and 9 months, enough gas would be produced to create the energy of an atomic bomb.

The human heart creates enough pressure when it pumps out of the body to squirt blood 30 feet.

A pig's orgasm lasts 30 minutes.

A cockroach will live nine days without its head

before it starves to death.

Banging your head against a wall uses 150 calories an hour.

The male praying mantis cannot copulate while its head is attached to its body. The female initiates sex by ripping the male's head off.

The flea can jump 350 times its body length. It's like a human jumping the length of a football pitch.

An octopus has over 27,000 taste buds.

Some lions mate over 50 times a day.

Butterflies taste with their feet.

The strongest muscle in the body is the tongue.

Right-handed people live, on average, nine years longer than left-handed people.

An ostrich's eye is bigger than its brain.

Starfish have no brains.

Titanic facts?

The construction of the ship went at such a fast pace that at least one worker was accidentally walled up in the hull and left to die.

Workers in Belfast almost stopped construction of the ship because the hull number 3909 04 seemed to spell out "NO POPE" when viewed in a mirror.

A cursed mummy that had already caused several deaths was in the cargo hold when the ship sank.

The *Titanic* was the first ship to use SOS as a distress call.

A tooth left overnight in a glass of Coca-Cola will dissolve.

Washing your feet with vodka cures foot odour.

You can turn vodka into mouthwash using a cup of vodka, 9 tablespoons of cinnamon and an airtight container to seal it up in for two weeks. After you strain out the cinnamon you have mouthwash.

After hearing screams from a Glasgow hotel room, a man broke in and found a naked woman tied to a bed. Her boyfriend was unconscious on the floor, dressed as Superman. He'd hit his head during the sex game and left her helpless.

The wax used to line the cups of instant noodles will build up in your internal organs causing serious problems later in life.

There was a brand of diet pills that contained the heads of tapeworms. Inside people's bodies they'd regenerate and the people would immediately begin to lose weight. The only way to get rid of the worms, once infested, is to starve for days then sit a bowl of warm milk in front of you and open your mouth. The hungry worms can smell it and will crawl up your throat and out into the milk.

The two about vodka are true.

CHAPTER TWENTY-THREE

Blind dates

The man who worked in the big Boots in Sauchiehall Street was getting tired of watching the nervous teenager wander around the store so he asked if he could help him. The boy stammered a little and the sales assistant pulled some condoms from behind the counter and asked if that was what he was looking for.

The teenager eventually said it was. The amused man told the boy not to worry, he was sure he'd do fine. He gave him some words of encouragement, wished him luck and told him with a wink, "I'm counting on you to become a regular customer." That evening as the young man approached the door of his new girlfriend's house he was thankful for the advice the man in the shop had given him, but his confidence quickly disappeared when he rang the bell and his girlfriend's father, the sales assistant, answered the door.

An attractive young woman was taking a shower one day and the doorbell started ringing. She jumped out to get it, but couldn't find a towel to wrap herself in. As she headed for the bedroom to grab something, she yelled: "Who's there?" The voice called out: "It's a blind man." The woman thought he wanted to sell some pencils, Jaycloths or something and stopped, realizing that she didn't have to get any of her clothes wet, he couldn't see her anyway. When she opened the door a wide-eyed man in grey overalls asked her "Eh, where do you want me to put your blinds?"

A man and his wife were supposed to go to a fancy-dress party together one Halloween, but when the time came to go the woman told him to go on without her, she had a terrible headache. The man reluctantly did, and the suspicious wife decided to see just how faithful her man really was. She put on a different costume and went to the party. When she got there and she saw her husband dancing with a young girl in a sexy costume she got even more suspicious, and she decided to really put him to the test. She danced with him and whispered that they should sneak into a bedroom.

She insisted they leave the masks on and had sex with him, then fuming, she ran home to wait for his return. When he got there she innocently asked if he'd enjoyed himself. He told her he hadn't. He said he'd had one dance with one of their son's teachers and that after a few minutes he and a couple of guys he met at the party had gone across the street to a pub to watch the football. He added, "The bloke who borrowed my costume said he had a really good time, though!"

A couple were celebrating an anniversary and had rented exactly the same room they had stayed in on their honeymoon. When they got there it was pretty much the same except for a little wear and tear. It had the round bed and mirrors on the ceiling just like their previous visit.

They had, however, added a little machine that would allow you to watch porn movies on the telly, and as his wife changed for bed the man decided to check it out. A few minutes into the second scene he realized it had been filmed in the room they were staying in, and had stayed in during their honeymoon. Then he realized it *was* their honeymoon.

Wee Davie had stayed out too late again and was afraid his wife would be angry. On the way home he decided he'd sneak in the window and ravish her before she had a chance to be angry or notice the time.

All went as planned and afterward he went downstairs to get a snack from the kitchen and saw his wife on the couch in the living room. "What are you doing down here?" he asked. "Ssssshhhh! Keep it down. Your mother's upstairs asleep in our bed!"

CHAPTER TWENTY-FOUR

This is the creepy scary one.
Every word is true.

A young girl returned from a night out with her friends in Rutherglen and she didn't want to disturb her sleeping sister, so she crept into the room and found her way in the darkness, undressed and slid into bed. The next morning when she awoke and turned to say something to her sister, she saw her mangled body on the blood-soaked bed. Written in her sister's blood on the wall were the words: "AREN'T YOU GLAD YOU DIDN'T TURN ON THE LIGHT?"

A young girl was babysitting, the children were in bed and she was watching TV when the phone rang. All the voice on the other end did was laugh. She listened for a minute then hung up. A few minutes later it happened again, she was very upset and called the police who told her there was really nothing they could do, but they'd trace the call if it happened again. After she got another call from the laughing voice, she hung up and the police immediately rang her and told her to get out of the house immediately, the calls were coming from the other phone upstairs, where he'd already murdered the children.

A man and woman went to Glasgow for their honeymoon, and checked into a room at a hotel. When they got to their room they both noticed a bad smell. The husband called down to reception and asked to speak to the manager. He explained that the room smelled very bad and they would like another room. The manager apologized and told the man that they were all booked because of a game at Hampden. He offered to send them to a restaurant of their choice for lunch, compliments of the hotel, and said he was going to send a maid up to their room to clean and to try and get rid of the stink.

After a nice lunch the couple went back to their room. When they walked in they could both still smell the same smell. Again the husband called reception and told the manager that the room still niffed really badly.

The manager told the man that they would try and find a room at another hotel. He called every big hotel in the city, but each was sold out because of the game. The manager told the couple that they couldn't find them a room anywhere, but they would try and clean the room again. The couple wanted to see a bit of Glasgow and do a little shopping anyway, so they said they would give them two hours to clean up and then they would be back.

When the couple had left, the manager and all of the cleaning staff went to the room to try and find what was making the room smell. They searched the entire room and found nothing, so the maids changed the sheets, changed the towels, took down the curtains and put new ones up, cleaned the carpet and cleaned the room again using the strongest cleaning stuff they had.

The couple came back two hours later to find the room still had a bad smell. The husband was so angry at this point, as this was on its way to wrecking his honeymoon, so he decided to find whatever this smell was himself and started tearing the entire room apart.

He pulled the mattress off the bed and under it he found the dead body of a woman.

It only takes one dead body under the mattress to spoil your whole honeymoon, eh?

How do I know that this one isn't true?

Who would honeymoon in Glasgow?

A young girl was left alone at home for the first time with only her dog to protect her, when she heard a bulletin on the radio about an inmate who had escaped from the nearby asylum. She immediately locked all the doors and went to bed. A dripping sound from the bathroom made it difficult to fall asleep and she reached down under her bed to make sure her faithful dog was by her side. He replied by licking her hand enthusiastically. The next morning when she woke up and went to the bathroom, she found her dog hanging from the shower nozzle, blood dripping from his torn throat. On the mirror, written in blood, were the words: "People can lick, too!"

One day a scrap metal worker fell feet-first into the crusher. His legs were pulped and his torso was hopelessly stuck. The paramedics said that if they pulled him out it would kill him, and if they left him there he'd die soon. They gave him some painkillers and his mates rang his wife. The woman ran to her husband, they exchanged a few words and a kiss, and then called for the machine to be turned back on.

An atheist who was training for the Olympics had been given special pool privileges at Glasgow University. Late one night he was considering the arguments a religious friend had been confronting him with as he climbed up to the board for a little late-night practice.

He stood on the board and prepared for a backward flip when he noticed the shadow he was casting on the wall formed a perfect cross in the partially-lit room. Shaken, he sat down on the board to think. As he sat there a maintenance worker came into the pool area and turned on the rest of lights and the diver saw that the pool had been drained.

A laden-down young woman returns to her car from a hard day's shopping in the Italian Centre and Princes Square. She had parked her car in the multi-storey car park in West Nile Street.

As she approaches the car she notices someone sitting in the back seat. She cautiously checks the number plate to see if it is indeed her car, as it is a popular model and colour. The car is indeed hers, and as she gets closer she sees that it's an old woman sitting in the back seat.

She asks the woman how and why she is sitting in her car. The old woman replies that she had been shopping with her son and family but felt ill and returned to the car to rest. She obviously had mistaken the young woman's car for her son's, as it was the same model and colour. The old woman then asks to be driven to a hospital, as she is still feeling unwell. The young woman agrees.

As she gets into the driver's seat something makes her very nervous about the situation, like wondering how the woman actually got into the locked car, and she asks the old woman if she is feeling well enough to direct her as she reverses the car out of the parking place. The old woman agrees, gets out of the car and proceeds to direct the reversing manoeuvre.

As soon as the young woman has the car out of the parking space she speeds out of the car park, leaving the old woman stranded. She then drives straight to the nearest police station and reports the incident.

A policeman then searched the car and found an axe concealed under the passenger seat.

The tale of "The Hairy-Armed Hitchhiker" goes back to the early 1800s. In those days, the well-disguised axe murderer was said to have awaited his victim in the back seat of a horse-drawn carriage.

More recently, the legend has resurfaced featuring a man in a nice suit whose briefcase turns out to be loaded with weapons. It is 200 years old and still going strong – proof that a good story never dies.

CHAPTER TWENTY-FIVE

This is the one where you look and act like an idiot

Lock the keys in the car? If you lock your keys in the car and the spare keys are at home, call home on your moby. Hold your phone about a foot from your car door and have the person at home press the unlock button, holding it near the phone at their end.

Your car will unlock. It saves someone from having to bring your keys to you or expensive taxis. Distance is no object. You could be hundreds of miles away, and if you can reach someone who has the other remote for your car, you can unlock the doors (or the boot).

It works fine. We tried it and it unlocked our car over the phone.

Aye, right.

CHAPTER TWENTY-SIX

Plutonic and other relationships

Pluto may have been cast out to the darkest reaches of the Solar System but will always be a friend to the Seven Dwarfs.

The Walt Disney Co. characters have issued a hard-hitting statement after the world's top astronomical body decided to relegate Pluto to the lowly status of a "dwarf planet".

School text books will have to be rewritten and Mickey Mouse's faithful companion is said by Disney insiders to be anguished over the fate of his planetary namesake.

But the Seven Dwarfs are not taking it lying down.

"Although we think it's DOPEY that Pluto has been downgraded to a dwarf planet, which has made some people GRUMPY and others just SLEEPY, we are not BASHFUL in saying we would be HAPPY if Disney's Pluto would join us as an eighth dwarf," they insisted.

"We think this is just what the DOC ordered and is nothing to SNEEZE at."

Pluto the dog made his debut in 1930, the same year that a 24-year-old American astronomer, Clyde Tombaugh, discovered what until now was called the ninth and outermost planet.

A white-gloved, yellow-shoed source close to Disney's top dog said: "I think the whole thing is goofy. Pluto has never been interested in astronomy before, other than maybe an occasional howl at the moon."

Mickey Mouse was unavailable for comment.

And have you heard about the seven levels of cocaine dependency?

Grumpy

Dopey

Sneezy

Sleepy

Bashful

Happy

And eventually

Doc

This nonsense reminded me of the episode in *Soap* where the gay son is rhyming off a list of historical characters who were gay. "Da Vinci was gay.

Michaelangelo was gay, Plato was gay". At this last his mother interrupted, saying incredulously, "Mickey Mouse's dog is gay?"

And speaking of soap, below is some correspondence which actually occurred between a Glasgow hotel's staff and one of its guests.

Dear Maid person,

Please do not leave any more of those little bars of soap in my bathroom since I have brought my own bath-sized Imperial Leather. Please remove the six unopened little bars from the shelf under the medicine chest and the other three in the shower soap dish. They are in my way.

Thank you,
David MacGregor

_____

Dear Room 635,

I am not your usual Maid person. She will be back tomorrow from her day off. I took the 3 hotel soaps out of the shower soap dish as you requested. The 6 bars on your shelf I took out of your way and put on top of your Kleenex dispenser in case you should change your mind. This leaves only the 3 bars I left today, as my instruction from the management is to leave 3 soaps daily. I hope this is satisfactory.

Kathy, Relief Maid person

Dear Maid person,

I hope you are my usual Maid person. Apparently Kathy did not tell you about my note to her concerning the little bars of soap. When I got back to my room this evening I found you had added 3 little Camays to the shelf under my medicine cabinet. I am going to be here in the hotel for two weeks and have brought my own bath-size Imperial Leather so I won't need those 6 little Camays which are on the shelf. They are in my way when shaving, brushing teeth, etc. Please remove them.

David MacGregor

Dear Mr MacGregor,

My day off was last Wednesday so the relief Maid person left 3 hotel soaps which we are instructed to do by the management. I took the 6 soaps which were in your way on the shelf and put them in the soap dish where your Imperial Leather was. I put the Imperial Leather in the medicine cabinet for your convenience. I didn't remove the 3 complimentary soaps which are always placed inside the medicine cabinet for all new arrivals and which you did not object to when you checked in on Monday. Please let me know if I can of further assistance.

Your regular Maid person,
Senga

———————————

Dear Mr MacGregor,

The assistant manager, Mr. Davidson, informed me this morning that you rang him last night and said you were unhappy with your Maid person service. I have assigned a new girl to your room. I hope you will accept my apologies for any past inconvenience. If you have any future complaints, please contact me so I can give it my personal attention. Call extension

1108 between 8am and 5pm.

Thank you,
Elaine Magillicuddy, Housekeeper

Dear Miss Magillicuddy,

It is impossible to contact you by phone since I leave the hotel for business at 7:45am and don't get back before 5:30 or 6pm. That's the reason I called Mr. Davidson last night. You were already off duty. I only asked Mr. Davidson if he could do anything about those little bars of soap. The new Maid person you assigned me must have thought I was a new arrival today, since she left another 3 bars of hotel soap in my medicine cabinet along with her regular delivery of 3 bars on the bathroom shelf. In just 5 days here I have accumulated 24 little bars of soap. Why are you doing this to me?

David MacGregor

Dear Mr MacGregor,

Your Maid person, Senga, has been instructed to stop delivering soap to your room and remove the extra soaps. If I can be of further assistance, please call extension 1108 between 8am and 5pm.

Thank you,
Elaine Magillicuddy, Housekeeper

———————————

Dear Mr. Davidson,

My bath-size Imperial Leather is missing. Every bar of soap was taken from my room including my own bath-size Imperial Leather. I came in late last night and had to get room service to bring me stupid wee soaps. I ask again, why are you doing this to me?

David MacGregor

———————————

Dear Mr MacGregor,

I have informed our housekeeper, Elaine Magillicuddy, of your soap problem. I cannot understand why there was no soap in your room since our Maid persons are instructed to leave 3 bars of soap each time they service a room. The situation will be rectified immediately. Please accept my apologies for the inconvenience.

Martin L. Davidson, Assistant Manager

———————————

Dear Mrs. Magillicuddy,

Who the fuck left 54 little bars of Camay in my room? I came in last night and found 54 little bars of soap. I don't want 54 little bars of Camay. I want my one fucking bar of bath-size Imperial Leather. Do you realise I have 54 bars of soap in here? All I want is my bath-size Imperial Leather. Please give me back my bath-size Imperial Leather.

David MacGregor

———————————

Dear Mr MacGregor,

You complained of too much soap in your room so I had them removed. Then you complained to Mr. Davidson that all your soap was missing so I personally returned them. The 24 Camays which had been taken and the 3 Camays you are supposed to receive daily. I don't know anything about the 4 wee bars you mention. Obviously your Maid person, Senga, did not know I had returned your soaps so she also brought 24 Camays plus the 3 daily Camays. I don't know where you got the idea that this hotel issues bath-size Imperial Leather. I was able to locate some bath-size Lifebuoy which I left in your room.

Elaine Magillicuddy, Housekeeper

———————————————

Dear Mrs Magillicuddy,

Just a short note to bring you up to date on my latest soap supplies. As of today I possess:

– on shelf under medicine cabinet, 18 Camay in 4 stacks of 4 and 1 stack of 2.

– on Kleenex dispenser, 11 Camay in 2 stacks of 4 and 1 stack of 3.

– on bedroom cabinet, 1 stack of 3 wee soaps which don't have a label, 1 stack of 4 hotel-size other wee soaps with a different label, and 8 Camay in 2 stacks of 4.

– inside medicine cabinet, 14 Camay in 3 stacks of 4 and 1 stack of 2.

– in shower soap dish, 6 Camay, very moist.

– on north east corner of the bath, 1 unidentified

wee soap, slightly used.

   – on north west corner of the bath, 6 Camays in 2 stacks of 3.

   – on bedroom window sill, 1 bath-sized Lifebuoy, which I hate.

Please ask Senga when she services my room to make sure the stacks are neatly piled and dusted. Also, please advise her that stacks of more than 4 have a tendency to topple over. May I suggest that my bedroom window sill is not in use, apart from the Lifebuoy, and will make an excellent spot for future soap deliveries. And to keep you further up to date, I have obtained another bar of bath-sized Imperial Leather which I am keeping in the hotel safe in order to avoid further misunderstandings. If you have access to this, please do not tell me.

David MacGregor.

CHAPTER TWENTY-SEVEN

A myth is a good as a mile

Recounting urban myths as though they had happened to you can improve your social standing immensely and make people like you and buy you drinks.

An urban myth is not just any apocryphal tale that is told as true. To qualify as an urban myth, a story must be officially sanctioned by the seven-member Urban Myth Committee of Glasgow University. Committee members are selected on the basis of academic achievement, pubic service (or possibly public service) and capacity for strong drink. Whenever a new president is elected, wee red flags are flown from every rooftop in Hillhead, while the ashes of the previous president are thrown into the Kelvin.

The story about the Maryhill gangs who drive with their lights off and shotgun drivers who flash them was written in 1875 by Charles Dickens.

The comparative rarity of the Maklouf-effigy £2 coins (the ones with the necklace) mean that they are much more valuable than the other coins, and if you place it in the freezer overnight, the cupro-nickel centre will pop out.

Every year, on the first Sunday in October, candle-light vigils are held in small towns around the world for the baby who was put in the microwave to dry.

The rumour of the rat in the bucket of Kentucky Fried Chicken in Bellshill was so distressing to Colonel Sanders that it led to his suicide in 1981.

The Paisley woman who originated the tale of the man who awoke in a hotel bath with his kidneys removed went on to write a folk song about how she came up with the idea. On the recording, she accompanied herself on acoustic guitar and harmonica, and was sued by Dylan for plagiarism. The song was a hit during a brief period in the winter of 1974-75, but only in Govan.

Most people relate to the story of the Oriental rat that was mistaken for a Chihuahua and adopted by a Blackhill family because, at one time or another, they have mistakenly adopted rats themselves.

Over 50% of all traffic on the Internet consists of urban myths.

POLICE WARNING

Police are warning all men who frequent clubs, parties and local pubs to be alert and stay cautious when offered a drink from any woman. Many females use a date rape drug on the market called 'Beer'. The drug is found in liquid form and available anywhere. It comes in bottles, cans, from taps and in large kegs.

Beer is used by female sexual predators at parties and bars to persuade their male victims to go home and have sex with them. A woman needs only to get a man to consume a few units of Beer and then simply ask him home for no-strings-attached sex. Men are rendered helpless by this approach.

After several Beers, men will often succumb to the desires to perform sexual acts on horrific-looking women to whom they would never normally be attracted.

After drinking Beer, men often awaken with only hazy memories of exactly what happened to them the night before, often with just a vague feeling that "something bad" occurred.

At other times these unfortunate men are swindled

out of their life savings, in a familiar scam known as "a relationship". In extreme cases, the female may even be shrewd enough to entrap the unsuspecting male into a longer form of servitude and punishment referred to as "marriage". Men are much more susceptible to this scam after Beer is administered and sex is offered by the predatory females. Please! Forward this warning to every male you know.

If you fall victim to this Beer and the women administering it, there are male support groups where you can discuss the details of your shocking encounter with similarly affected, like-minded men. For the support group nearest you, just look up "golf courses" or "public houses" in the phone book.

Doctors are blaming a rare electrical imbalance in the brain for the bizarre death of a chess player whose head exploded in the middle of a championship game. The normal chants of, "Come and take a pawn if you think you're hard enough!", and, "Anatoly Karpov! He's a wanker! He's a wanker!" were silenced as bits of bone and hair showered the crowd.

No one else was hurt in the fatal explosion but four players and three officials at the Glasgow Masters' Chess Championships were sprayed with blood and brain matter when Snakehips McGunnagle's head suddenly blew apart. Experts say he suffered from a condition called Hyper-Cerebral Electrosis or HCE.

"He was deep in concentration with his eyes focused on the board," said Snakehips' opponent, Vladimir MacDobrynin. "All of a sudden his hands flew to his temples and he screamed in pain. Everyone looked up from their games, startled by the noise. Then, as if someone had put a bomb in his cranium, his head popped like a melon hit with a hammer."

Incredibly, Snakehips' is not the first case in which a person's head has spontaneously exploded. Five people are known to have died of HCE in the last 25 years. The most recent death occurred in 1991, when English psychic Barbara Nicole's skull burst. Miss Nicole's story was reported by newspapers worldwide, including the *Herald*, which ran with the headline, "She Didny See That One Coming, Ha Ha!"

"HCE is an extremely rare physical imbalance," said Dr. Peedie Penis, famed neurologist and expert on the human brain, who did the autopsy on the brilliant chess master. "It is a condition in which the circuits of the brain become overloaded by the body's own electricity. The explosions happen during periods of intense mental activity when lots of current is surging through the brain. Victims are highly intelligent people with great powers of concentration. Both Miss Nicole and Snakehips were intense people who tended to keep those cerebral circuits overloaded. In a way, it could be said they were literally too clever for their own good."

Although Dr. Penis says there are probably many undiagnosed cases, he hastens to add that very few people die from HCE. "Most people who have it will never know. At this point, medical science still doesn't know much about HCE. And since fatalities are so rare it will probably be years before research money becomes available."

In the meantime, the doctor urges people to take it easy and not think too hard for long periods of time. "Take frequent relaxation breaks when you're doing things that take lots of mental focus," he recommends.

Although HCE is very rare, it can kill. Dr. Penis says knowing you have the condition can greatly improve your odds of surviving it. A "yes" answer to any three of the following eight questions could mean that you have HCE:

Does your head sometimes ache when you think too hard? (Head pain can indicate overloaded brain circuits.)

Do you ever hear a faint ringing or humming sound in your ears? (It could be the sound of electricity in the skull cavity.)

Do you sometimes find yourself unable to get a thought out of your head? (This is a possible sign of too much electrical activity in the cerebral cortex.)

Do you spend more than five hours a day reading, balancing your cheque book, wondering about Motherwell's chances in the Scottish Cup, or other thoughtful activity? (A common symptom of HCE is a tendency to overuse the brain.)

When you get angry or frustrated do you feel pressure in your temples? (Friends of people who died of HCE say the victims often complained of head pressure in times of strong emotion.)

Do you ever eat too much ice cream, Midget Gems or other sweeties? (A craving for sugar is typical of people with too much electrical pressure in the cranium.)

Do you tend to analyze yourself too much? (HCE sufferers are often introspective, "over-thinking" their lives.)

Do you ever unzip your head with the zip at the back?

Here is the advice of Dr Peedie Penis if you are doing even any one of the above:

"Don't, ya eejit".

Idiots in the office are just as hazardous to your health as cigarettes, caffeine or greasy food, an eye-opening new study reveals. In fact, those fools can kill you!

Stress is one of the top causes of heart attacks, and working with stupid people on a daily basis is one of the deadliest forms of stress, according to researchers at Glasgow University Medical Centre, in the Western Infirmary.

The author of the study, Dr. Wilma Anderson, says her team studied 500 heart attack patients, and were puzzled to find 62% had relatively few of the physical risk factors commonly blamed for heart attacks.

"Then we questioned them about lifestyle habits, and almost all of these low-risk patients told us they worked with people so stupid they can barely find their way from the car park to their office. And their heart attack came less than 12 hours after having a major confrontation with one of these oafs.

"One woman had to be rushed to hospital after her assistant shredded important company tax documents instead of copying them. A man told us he collapsed at his desk because the woman in the next cubicle kept asking him for correction fluid. This was for her computer monitor.

"You can cut back on smoking or improve your

diet," Dr. Anderson says, "but most people have very poor coping skills when it comes to stupidity. They feel there's nothing they can do about it, so they just internalize their frustration until they finally explode."

Stupid fellow-workers can also double or triple someone's work load, she explains. "Many of our subjects feel sorry for the drooling idiots they work with, so they try to cover for them by fixing their mistakes. One poor woman spent a week rebuilding client records because a typist put them all in the recycle bin of her computer and then emptied it. She thought it meant the records would be recycled and used again."

Dr Anderson's advice regarding these idiots is simple. She says, "Kill them, they deserve it."

CHAPTER TWENTY-EIGHT

No fatwahs re Saddam, please, or burning
crosses on my lawn re Harry.
These are myths. Perhaps.

Incidentally, what do you call a Muslim flying an aeroplane?

The pilot, you racist.

Saddam Hussein has been caught with his trousers down – literally. A shocking 1968 porn film has surfaced at his trial, in which the flamboyant former leader appears performing raunchy homosexual acts.

The image quality of the grainy 16mm film is poor, but experts who've taken a close look at the hairy-chested actor are "100 per cent certain" it is a younger, trimmer Saddam.

"There is no doubt in my mind that this is Saddam. There's no mistaking those eyes and that distinctive nose," declares Hussein biographer Sadiq al-Sabah, who has seen the eye-popping footage first-hand.

It may be hard to believe that a man who led one

of the most powerful nations in the Middle East once acted in blue movies, but to anyone familiar with how reckless and sexually promiscuous Saddam was in his youth, when he lived in Auchenshuggle, this will come as no surprise. It's also a known fact that the young, desperate lad did anything for money.

"Saddam appeared in as many as 85 of these films under a variety of stage names, most frequently Omar Studdif," reveals the researcher.

Still photographs from the sizzling X-rated film, La'iba al-Waladaani (The Two Boys Played), were leaked to a news magazine after authorities found it amid a stash of illicit porn in the desk of a recently deceased Glasgow MP.

But rumours that Saddam appeared in gay porn films in his younger days have dogged him for decades and almost torpedoed his political career when he was a rising star in the Baath Socialist party.

"He was able to squelch the rumours in the past, but now it looks like we have found the smoking gun," says a State Department source.

Al-Sabah claims that Saddam, then a struggling law student, acted in porn to make ends meet, as it were, and because he was addicted to gay sex.

In the newly uncovered 86-minute prison movie, set in Barlinnie, Saddam, then just 34, plays a naive young man who is wrongly convicted and sent to jail.

He is initiated into homosexuality by a series of older and more experienced cons.

"Saddam's acting in the picture is actually quite good," al-Sabah notes. "One scene, in which he buries his face in a pillow and cries, is so touching you can almost forget you are watching a low-budget sexploitation film."

The trial continues.

Harry Potter is the creation of a former English teacher who promotes witchcraft and Satanism. In the first book, Harry is a 13-year-old wizard. Her creation openly blasphemes Jesus and God and promotes sorcery, seeking revenge upon anyone who upsets them by giving you examples (quoting author and title references) of spells, rituals, and demonic powers. I think the problem is that parents have not reviewed the material.

The name seems harmless enough – Harry Potter. But that is where it all ends. Let me give you a few quotes from some of the influenced readers themselves: "The Harry Potter books are cool 'cause they teach you all about magic and how you can use it to control people and get revenge on your enemies," said Bearsden pupil, 10-year-old Craig Davies, a recent convert to the New Satanic Order of the

Black Circle. "I want to learn the Cruciatus Curse, to make my muggle science teacher suffer 'cause she's a pig." (A muggle is a non-believer in magic.)

Or how about the really young and innocent impressionable mind of a 6-year-old when asked about her favourite character? "Hermione is my favourite, because she's smart and has a beauty wee kitten," said 6-year-old Jessica MacDonald of North Kelvinside. "Jesus died because He was weak and stupid."

And here is Ashley, a 9-year-old, the average age of a Harry Potter reader: "I used to believe in what they taught us at Sunday School," said Ashley, conjuring up an ancient spell to summon Cerebus, the three-headed hound of Hell. "But the Harry Potter books showed me that magic is real, something I can learn and use right now, and that the Bible is nothing but boring lies."

Or how about a quote from a High Priest of Satanism: "Harry is an absolute devil-send to our cause," said High Priest Joe Egan of the First Church of Satan in Sauchiehall Street. "An organization like ours thrives on new blood – no pun intended – and we've had more applicants than we can handle lately. And, of course, practically all of them are virgins, which is brill." (Since 1995, applicants to Satanic worship have increased from around 100,000 to 1.4

million children and young adults.)

I think I can offer you an explanation as to why this is happening. Children have been bombarded with action, adventure, thrills and scares to the point that authors and film makers can produce nothing new to give them the next high. Parents have neglected to see what their children are reading and doing, and simply seem satisfied that Wee Peem is interested in reading.

Still not convinced? I will leave you with something to let you make up your own mind – a quote from the author herself, J. K. Rowling, describing the objections of Christian reviewers to her writings: "I think it's absolute rubbish to protest about children's books on the grounds that they are luring children to Satan," Rowling told a Glasgow *Evening News* reporter in a recent interview. "People should be praising them for that! These books guide children to an understanding that the weak, idiotic Son Of God is a living hoax who will be humiliated when the rain of fire comes, while we, Satan's faithful servants, laugh and cavort in victory."

CHAPTER TWENTY-NINE

Wee boys and other creatures

There is a prevailing myth in Glasgow that all wee boys are smart-arsed experts in repartee, not to mention banter and talking back.

There is the standard story of the chap parking his car outside the football and being asked by mini-blackmailers: "Watch yer car, mister?" This is, of course, an implied threat that if you don't give them a quid or whatever the going rate is, that something nasty, like disappearance, especially if you are in Ibrox or Parkhead, might just happen to your vehicle.

The story goes that a guy points somewhat condescendingly to the Dobermann/ Rottweiler/Irish Wolfhound in the back of the car and says: "I think my dog can watch my car for me."

I can find no one to which this has ever happened but the mythical replies grow year on year. So far I have heard:

"Yer dug pits oot fires, does it?"

"Yer dug blaws up tyres, does it?"

"Yer dug fixes broken headlights, does it?"

and the classic, "Paints oot scratches, does it?"

The new one this year is, "Worth much, that dug?" which, given that people are spending a fortune on the above breeds, really is pretty smart. You lose your car and your pet.

The other variation I have been told about was a couple of smart kids actually juggling bricks, a bit like saying, "I hope I don't drop a brick on it."

Throw them a rag and say: "Wash the windows and meet me here after the game."

A couple of guys are out one night in town on the bevvy, with a few drugs thrown in. They're highly illegally driving their car back to Easterhouse in the middle of the night, when something runs in front of the car and on to the other side of the road. For whatever reason, possibly because they are both steamboats and possibly because they have both seen *The Hobbit*, they agree that it was a goblin, and they pull the car over and attempt to apprehend the goblin in the interest of science.

They manage to catch the goblin and put it in the boot of the car. They get home to one of their houses, lock the goblin in the kitchen, and then pass out. When they awake, they wonder if the evening's events were just a dream, a drug trip, or if there is in fact a goblin in the kitchen. They open the kitchen to find a frightened 5-year-old boy who has Down's Syndrome. They called the police to report the boy, and end up being heroes because the boy had been missing for days and his well-off parents were frantic. They received a decent-sized cash reward for his safe return.

Two guys were walking in the Campsies when they came across a big hole. The two saw that it was a deep hole, but wanted to know how deep, as you do. They threw stones in and then bigger stones. When they heard nothing hit the ground, the two decided to use something heavier and bigger. Just at the edge of a farm field they found an old railway sleeper. It took both of them to lift it, but they finally got it to the hole and threw it in. Just then a goat came running towards the men at full speed. It went past the two, jumped up into the air and into the hole. The two looked at each other in amazement. Behind the men, a farmer came out from behind a dyke and said, "Have you seen my goat?" The two men looked at him and said, "Aye, we did. It jumped into this hole." The farmer looked around and then said, "No, it couldn't have been my goat. It's tied to a sleeper."

A cat that had helped itself to some salmon mousse, prepared for an upcoming dinner party, later turns up dead in the garden. The hostess, fearing her dish is poisonous, convinces her guests to rush to the Western and get their stomachs pumped. Later that evening a neighbour comes over to apologize for backing his car over the cat, which ran away injured.

For the final exam in a philosophy class at Strathclyde, the professor took his chair and placed it on top of his desk. He gives each student a blank piece of paper and said: "Prove to me that this chair does not exist". Most papers handed in were essays explaining how nothing was real or references to ancient philosophers. The paper which received top marks was just two words long:

"Whit chair?"

CHAPTER THIRTY

Bus pass corner

An elderly lady went to the bar in a pub in Dumbarton and got a packet of potato crisps. She sat down at a nearby table and started to read a paper. Soon a young man came and sat down at her table. He lifted the potato crisps, opened them, and started to eat. The lady just watched the man eat the potato crisps, not wanting to cause any trouble. He noticed her watching him, then he offered her a crisp. She jerked it out of his hand and slowly started eating. She continued to stare. As soon the man was finished, he got up, put the empty bag on the bar, and walked away, staring back at her. She mumbled to herself, "Young people think they can do anything." She finished reading the newspaper, rose, and then noticed that under her newspaper was her bag of potato crisps.

An elderly couple went doon the watter for the weekend. While on the boat, the man began to get a little seasick and leaned over the edge to throw up, losing his false teeth while doing so. He was pretty upset about the incident, but his wife couldn't stop laughing about it. As a joke, she removed her own dentures and took them to her husband exclaming, "Hey, look what I caught!" Her husband put in the dentures and noticed that they didn't fit. He took the teeth out and threw them overboard, shook his head and said to his wife, "Those wurny mine."

CHAPTER THIRTY-ONE

A mythcellany

At Glasgow airport the baggage handlers find a dead dog in a pet-shipping container. The airport employees decide to take up a collection and send one of the workers to buy a lookalike dog to replace it, as they think its death might be their fault. When the owner comes to claim it, she opens the pet container and the replacement dog jumps out and licks her face. The woman faints. She had been shipping her dead dog home for burial.

As part of an exam on solutions, a Strathclyde professor asks his students how to determine the height of a building using a barometer. Some of his students gave obvious answers like using formulas, timing the fall of the barometer from the roof to the ground, tying a string from the barometer and lowering it to the ground then measuring the string, measuring the side of the building in units of "one barometer". The professor ruled all of these solutions unacceptable. The student that received the highest mark in the exam was able to answer the question in one sentence: "Give the barometer to the man who designed the building for the information."

A professor who was famous for his creative exam questions handed out the final exam to his students. The exam had only one question: "What is courage?" The top mark given on that particular exam was to a quiet young man who wrote: "This is."

A student in a very large class didn't stop working on his exam when the professor called, "Time up." When he went up to turn it in, the professor said he needn't bother, he'd already failed. The student looked at the large stack of exams on the desk and asked "Do you know who I am?" The professor replied that he didn't, and the student stuck his exam in the middle of the pile and said: "Good."

A man who was tired of having his motors broken into specifically asked for no radio when he bought his new car. He put a sign in the windscreen that said in large letters: "NO RADIO". One day he returned to it to find the window broken anyway. Beside his sign he found a note that read: "Just checking."

A student stops by the prof's office and finds that the professor has stepped out for a moment, leaving an unguarded pile of the next day's final examinations on his desk. The student quickly steals one of the exams and disappears. Before issuing the exam papers, however, the professor counts them and notices that one is missing. He cuts an eighth of an inch off the bottom of every exam paper prior to distributing them to the class, then fails the student with the long one.

This next apparently really happened in Bearsden.

A golfer was angry at his poor playing. He'd hit several balls into the pond on the eighteenth hole. Crimson with frustration and embarrassment, he flung his golf bag into the pond and stormed off the course in front of a crowd of club mates trying not to snigger. A few minutes later, with the crowd watching, he returned to the pond, fished out his bag with the greenkeeper's rake, retrieved his car keys from the bag and then threw the bag back into the pond.

A while back, during the construction of the Red Road flats, a worker was having a very hard day. He was being ordered to do work all over the place every second without a break. After eight straight hours of non-stop work, he was extremely tired. A Health and Safety nightmare. The foreman came up to him and told him that a piece of plywood needed to be removed from the roof. The worker grabbed the ladder and climbed to the roof. He had to be careful because the plywood was still in good condition. As he started walking back towards the ladder, he started to worry. He knew he was on a very tall building, and that if he fell it would kill him. So he started to pay more attention to his feet. The weight of the plywood shifted. The worker lost his balance, and fell off the roof. After a moment of panic, he noticed his fall had slowed. The plywood was acting like a parachute, and he was able to safely land on the ground.

A modern legend tells of a woman from Glasgow who visits Lourdes, famous for its stories of miraculous cures. Although in good health, the woman feels tired on the hot day of her visit, and she sits down in an empty wheelchair to rest, then falls asleep. Waking up when a priest arrives to bless the visitors, the woman jumps up from the chair and is immediately surrounded by a crowd screaming: "It's a miracle!" In the excitement, the woman was knocked to the ground and her leg was broken.

A Newton Mearns resident called the fire brigade to request assistance in removing her cat from a tree. The fire brigade responded with a rescue van which had an extension ladder. The tree, however, was too tall and willowy, if a poplar can be willowy, to support the weight of the extension ladder. Rather than send men back to the fire station to bring the aerial ladder truck, one of the firemen suggested an alternative course of action. Two of the firemen supported the ladder while a third climbed high enough to tie a rope around the tree about halfway up.

The other end of the rope was tied to the tow bar, and the van was slowly driven forward, forcing the tree to bend over. One fireman was poised to grab the cat as soon as it was within his reach.

The knot securing the rope to the tow bar slipped free.

The cat was last seen, airborne and yowling, heading towards Prestwick.

And finally, the myth of bottled water.

Evian is "naive" spelled backwards, because people who pay two quid for a bottle of water are.